The English Civil War
1642-51

John Barratt

𝕻artizan 𝕻ress
1992

D1221850

© John Barratt 1992
Maps © Derek Stone
Original illustrations by Neil Wright

Art Editor: Hawk Norton
Typeset by Portobello Press Ltd.
69-71 Scrubs Lane, London NW10 6QU

ISBN 0 946525 99 4

Published by Partizan Press, military book specialists.
26 Cliffsea Grove, Leigh on Sea, Essex SS9 1NQ

The
BRITISH ISLES
During the English Civil Wars.

Auldearn ×
INVERNESS

ABERDEEN
Justice Mills

SCOTLAND

× Kilsyth   Dunbar
EDINBURGH

CARLISLE   DURHAM

Marston Moor ×   YORK   HULL
Adwalton Moor ×
× Preston

IRELAND

DUBLIN
Rathmines

CHESTER   Winnington
Rowton Heath   × Bridge   LINCOLN   × Winceby
NEWARK
Nantwich   NOTTINGHAM   KINGS LYNN
SHREWSBURY   LEICESTER   NORWICH

Worcester   NORTHAMPTON   IPSWICH
Powicke Bridge   × Naseby   COLCHESTER

WALES   Edgehill   OXFORD
GLOUCESTER   LONDON
CARDIFF   CANTERBURY
St Fagans   BRISTOL
× Newbury   DOVER
Langport ×   SALISBURY   WINCHESTER
SOUTHAMPTON
EXETER   PORTSMOUTH
Braddock Down ×
Lostwithiel ×   PLYMOUTH

DS-92

The English Civil War 1642–51

The Civil War was one of the bloodiest and most influential episodes of British history. The pages which follow attempt to describe the men, and their arms and equipment, who fought for King or Parliament in those turbulent days 350 years ago.

A true and exact Relation of the

manner of his Maiesties setting up of His

Standard at *Nottingham*, on Munday the
22. of August 1642.

First, The forme of the Standard, as it is here figured, and who were present at the advancing of it

Secondly, The danger of setting up of former Standards, and the damage which ensued thereon.

Thirdly, A relation of all the Standards that ever were set up by any King.

Fourthly, the names of those Knights who are appointed to be the Kings Standard-bearers. With the forces that are appoynted to guard it.

Fifthly, The manner of the Kings comming first to *Coventry*.

Sixtly, The *Cavalieres* resolution and dangerous threats which they have uttered, if the King concludes a peace without them, or hearkens unto his great Councell the Parliament : Moreover how they have shared and divided *London* amongst themselves already.

Nottingham.

Chronology

1642

August 22	King Charles I raises his Standard at Nottingham; Civil War formally begins.
September 23	Prince Rupert wins cavalry action at Powicke Bridge
October 12	King leaves Shrewsbury on march to take London
October 23	Battle of Edgehill; tactical Royalist victory
November 13	Royalist advance halted at Turnham Green
November 29	King withdraws; establishes H.Q. at Oxford

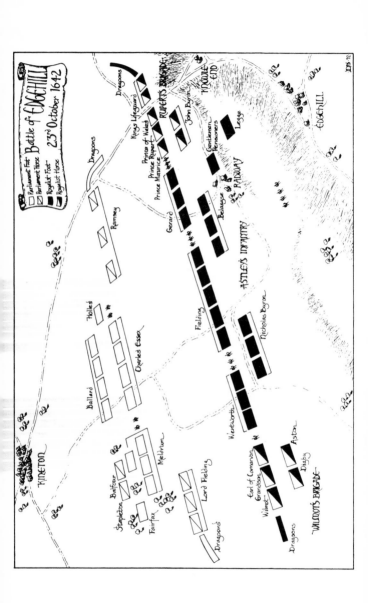

Battle of EDGEHILL
23rd October 1642

Parliament Foot
Parliament Horse
Royalist Foot
Royalist Horse

KINETON

Stapleton
Balfour
Ballard
Holles
Fairfax
Meldrum
Charles Essex
Lord Fielding
Dragons

Dragons
Ramsay
Dragons

Wentworth
Fielding
Gerard
Prince Maurice
Prince Rupert
Prince of Wales
Kings Lifeguard
John Byron
Rupert's Brigade
TYSOE END

ASTLEY'S INFANTRY
Nicholas Byron
Belasise
RADWAY
Gentlemen Pensioners
Legge

Earl of Carnarvon
Grandison
Wilmot
Digby
Aston
WILMOT'S BRIGADE
Dragons

EDGEHILL

KBS 92

1643

January 19	Cornish Royalist victory at Braddock Down
January 23	Sir Thomas Fairfax takes Leeds and Wakefield for Parliament
March 19	Narrow Royalist victory at Hopton Heath
March 30	Northern Royalist victory at Seacroft Moor
April 21	Rupert takes Lichfield
April 27	Earl of Essex occupies Reading for Parliament
May 16	Cornish Royalist victory at Stratton
June 30	Victory at Adwalton Moor gives Royalists control of much of North
July 5	Narrow Royalist victory at Lansdown over Sir William Waller
July 13	Waller decisively defeated at Roundway Down
July 26	Prince Rupert storms Bristol

July 28	Cromwell wins action at Gainsborough
August 10 – September 5	King fails to take Gloucester
September 20	Royalists fail to destroy Essex's Army at First Battle of Newbury
September 25	Parliament signs Solemn League and Covenant alliance with Scots
October 11	Cromwell wins action at Winceby; Royalists abandon siege of Hull

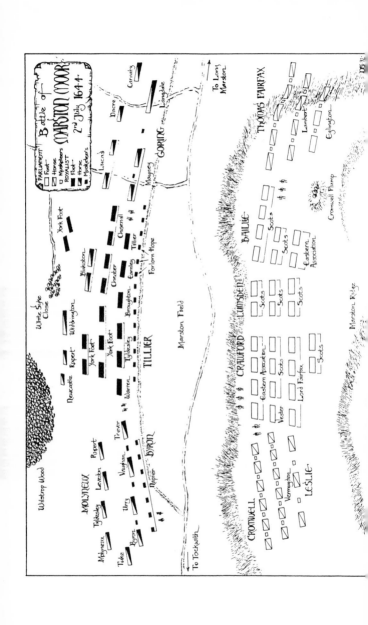

1644

January 19	Scots Army invades England
January 25	Royalist troops returned from Ireland defeated at Nantwich
March 21	Prince Rupert relieves Newark
March 29	Waller defeats Hopton at Cheriton, ending Royalist offensive in the South
May 18	Rupert begins march to conquer Lancashire and relieve York
June 29	King defeats Waller at Cropredy Bridge
July 2	Rupert and Northern Royalists smashed at Marston Moor. North effectively lost for King
September 1	Montrose, leading Royalist revolt in Scotland, wins battle of Tippermuir
September 3	Essex's army surrenders to King at Lostwithiel
September 13	Montrose wins battle of Justice Mills
October 27	Parliament fails to defeat Royalists at Second Battle of Newbury
December 19	House of Commons pass Self-Denying Ordnance, paving way for New Model Army

THE DESCRIPTION OF THE ARMIES OF HORSE AND FOOT OF HIS MAJESTIES, AND S.r Thomas Fairfax his Excellency, as they were drawn up severall bodies, at the Battaile at NASBYE the Fowerteenth day of June 1645

THE
Kings Cabinet opened

OR,

CERTAIN PACKETS

OF SECRET

LETTERS & PAPERS

Written with the Kings own Hand
and taken in his Cabinet at *Nasby-Field*,
JUNE 14. 1 6 4 5.

By Victorious Sr. *Thomas Fairfax*;

Wherein many mysteries of State, tending to the
Justification of that C A U S E, for which
Sir *Thomas Fairfax* joyned battell that
memorable day are clearly laid open;

Together, with some Annotations thereupon.

Published by speciall Oder of the *Parliament*.

L O N D O N,

Printed for *Robert Bostock*, dwelling in *Pauls* Church-
yard, at the Sign of the Kings-head, 1 6 4 5.

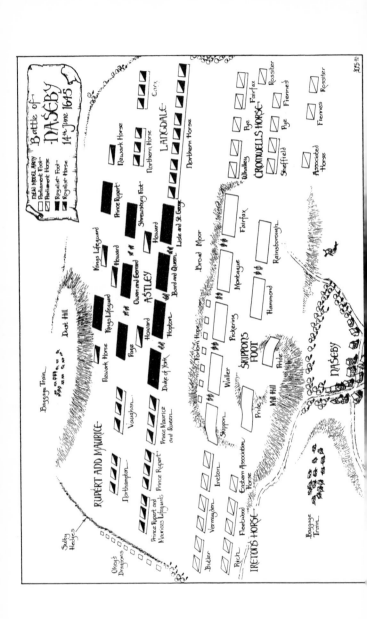

Battle of NASEBY
14th June 1645

NEW MODEL ARMY
☐ Parliament Foot
☐ Parliament Horse
■ Royalist Foot
◪ Royalist Horse

RUPERT AND MAURICE

Baggage Train

Sulby Hedges

Okey's Dragoons

Dust Hill

Newark Horse

King's Lifeguard
King's Lifeguard
Howard
Page
Howard
Duke of York

Northampton
Vaughan
Prince Rupert
Prince Maurice and Queens
Prince Rupert and Maurices Lifeguards

Prince Rupert
Howard
Owen and Everard
Hopton

ASTLEY

Shrewsbury Foot
Lisle and St George
Bard and Queens

Newark Horse
Northern Horse
Cary

LANGDALE

Northern Horse

Broad Moor

Mill Hill

Torburn Hope
Waller
Skippon
Pride

SKIPPON'S FOOT
Pickering
Pride

Fairfax
Montague
Hammond
Rainsborough

Whalley
Bye
Fairfax

CROMWELL'S HORSE

Sheffield
Pye
Fiennes

Rossiter

Associated Horse
Fiennes
Rossiter

IRETON'S HORSE

Butler
Vermuyden
Ireton
Eastern Association Horse
Rich
Fleetwood

Baggage Train

NASEBY

1645

February 2   Montrose defeats Campbells
at Inverlochy

April 4   New Model Army formed

May 9   Montrose defeats Urry at Auldearn

May 30   Prince Rupert storms Leicester

June 14   King's main field army destroyed
at Naseby

July 2   Montrose defeats Baillie at Alford

July 10   Western Royalist Army defeated
at Langport

August 15   Montrose wins battle of Kilsyth;
briefly controls much of Scotland

September 10   Prince Rupert surrenders Bristol

September 13   Montrose defeated at Philliphaugh;
never again a serious threat

September 26   Royalist cavalry defeated
at Rowton Heath

1646

February 16	Western Royalists defeated at Torrington
March 12	Hopton surrenders Western Royalist forces to Fairfax
March 21	Last Royalist field army surrenders at Stow on the Wold
May 5	King Charles surrenders to Scots
June 24	Oxford surrenders

1647

March 16	Surrender of Harlech Castle, last remaining Royalist garrison
December 26	King makes alliance with Scots

1648

March 23	Colonel Poyer declares for King in South Wales
May 21	Royalist rising in Kent, followed by others elsewhere

June 14	Fairfax lays siege to Colchester
July 8	Scots under Hamilton invade England
July 11	Cromwell takes Pembroke
August 17-19	Cromwell defeats Scots in series of engagements around Preston
August 28	Colchester surrenders; end of Second War

1649

January 30	King Charles I executed
September 12	Cromwell begins conquest of Ireland with storm of Drogheda

1650

September 3	Cromwell defeats Scots at Dunbar

1651

September 3	Cromwell defeats Charles II at Worcester; effective end of Civil Wars.

N.º 6

N.º 5

N.º 4

Figu: 8
Cap: 8
Par: 4

The Armies

Both King and Parliament maintained a number of field armies during the war. The principal Royalist army, based on that which had fought at Edgehill, is generally known as the "Oxford Army", from its being based at the King's headquarters in that city for most of the war. Besides this, the Royalists maintained a number of regional forces, including the famous army formed around the Cornish foot, commanded by Sir Ralph Hopton, and the Northern Royalist army commanded by the Earl of Newcastle.

From 1642-44, the principal Parliamentarian army was that under the command of its Lord General, the Earl of Essex. There was also the force, at one point called the Army of the Western Association, led by Sir William Waller, the Northern forces under Lord Fairfax, and the powerful Army of the Eastern Association, with which Cromwell served.

Regional forces were maintained until the end of the war, but in 1645, the "central" Parliamentarian armies were re-organised into the New Model Army. Despite its later fame, there was nothing especially unique about this army. The Royalists were also attempting a "re-modelling" at the same time, with very little success, and the Scots re-modelled their own forces in 1647. Parliament's troops soon dropped "New Model" from their title, and from 1647 it was generally just referred to as "the Army".

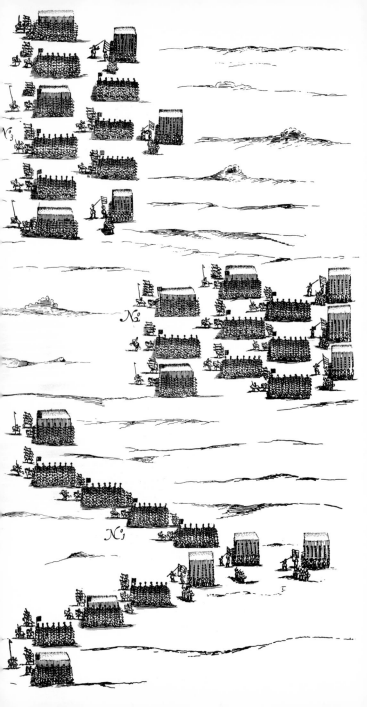

The Commanders

Although the officers and generals of both sides in the Civil Wars are often described as amateurs, and this was indeed true of many, including Cromwell himself, others had had considerable military experience on the Continent. They included large numbers of professional soldiers, whose services were eagerly sought by both sides, despite the somewhat flexible loyalties which such men sometimes displayed. As will be seen, the leading commanders of both sides included a mixture of both amateur and professional.

CHARLES I.
King of England, Scotland,
France & Ireland, &c.

HONI SOIT QUI MAL Y PENSE

DIEU ET MON DROIT

Royalist

King Charles I (1600-49)

The King had had no military experience prior to the outbreak of war, when he automatically became Captain General of the Royalist forces. His unfortunate mixture of weakness and stubborness, both usually displayed at the wrong time, were to have disastrous effects for the Royalist cause. Though Charles was to display considerable personal courage, albeit mainly of a passive kind, he displayed little evidence of generalship or the ability to control his generals.

CONTEMPORARY WOODCUT SHOWING PRINCE RUPERT
ON HIS WAY FROM DAVENTRY TO BIRMINGHAM

Prince Rupert (1619-82)

Nephew of King Charles, Rupert, despite his youth, had some military experience on the Continent prior to his arrival in England in 1642, and had made a keen study of the art of war. His appointment as General of Horse, coupled with Rupert's own prickly intolerant nature, made the Prince enemies among his fellow Royalists from the beginning. He proved to be an excellent leader of horse, certainly up to brigade level.

An energetic if tactless administrator, the Prince's capacity for higher command proved to be limited. The Battle of Marston Moor was lost in part because of his tactless handling of the Northern Royalist commanders, and his appointment in November 1644 as General of the Oxford Army proved to be a failure. Any chance of the Prince reviving the Royalist war-effort was frustrated by his many enemies.

William Cavendish, Earl of Newcastle (1592-1676)

It was said of Newcastle that he "had the misfortune to have somewhat of the poet in him", and that he "liked the pomp and absolute authority of a general" but not the substantial part, and fatigue". However his standing as the leading Royalist magnate in the North made his appointment on the outbreak of war as General of the Northern Counties inevitable. Lacking military experience himself, Newcastle was wise enough, at least, to appoint a team of professional soldiers to key positions, though he lacked the decisiveness necessary to use them to full effect.

Ralph, Lord Hopton (1598-1652)

With his motto of "I will Strive to Serve my Soveraigne King", Hopton, who had military experience prior to the Civil Wars, was to prove one of the most capable of the Royalist generals. In 1642-43, leading the Western Royalist army built around the redoubtable Cornish foot, he won a series of remarkable victories as he fought his way through to link up with the King's forces around Oxford. Seriously injured in a powder explosion after Lansdown, Hopton never recovered his old flair. Defeated by Waller at Cheriton, in March 1644, Hopton took something of a back seat until towards the end of the war, when he took command once more of the Western Royalist army in their last hopeless operations against the New Model.

Lord George Goring (1608-1657)

The "wild card" in the Royalist pack, Goring was both an ambitious, self-seeking, unscrupulous intriguer and libertine, and on his good days arguably the best commander of horse in the Royalist armies. An experienced veteran of the Continental Wars, Goring distinguished himself commanding horse in the North, at Marston Moor and the Second Battle of Newbury. Later he bitterly resented Rupert's authority, and proved a disappointment in independent command in the West. Despite steadily being undermined by drink and ill-health, Goring showed flashes of his old brilliance to the end, and was described by Richard Bulstrode, one of his officers, as "without dispute as good an officer as any that served the King, and the most dextrous in any sudden emergency that I have seen."

James Graham, 1st Marquis of Montrose (1612-50)

Montrose is one of the great romantic figures of the Civil wears, his attitude supposedly typified by his famous verse;

> "He either fears his fate too much,
>   Or his deserts are small,
>   That puts it not unto the touch,
>   To win or lose it all"

In fact, Montrose's earlier career had been somewhat more ambivalent than this suggests, and his skills as a general have sometimes been overstated. But the dramatic, if transient, Royalist successes in Scotland in 1644-45 owe much to his leadership and skills in for a time banding together many of the disparate elements who opposed the Covenanting regime. Montrose's chief military weakness lay in a consistent failure to appreciate the importance of adequate reconnaissance, which led both to his defeat at Philliphaugh, and his final overthrow at Carbisdale in 1650.

Robert Earle of Essex his Exellence
Lord Generall of the Parli.^{mts} Army etc:
lately deceased

Parliamentarian

Robert Deveraux,
3rd Earl of Essex (1591–1646)

Essex had served in the Palatinate and the Cadiz Expedition of 1625. After being second-in-command of the English armies during the Scots Wars, he was appointed as Captain-General of the Parliamentarian Armies on the outbreak of Civil War.

Essex proved a less than successful general. Though his gesture in taking his coffin with him on his opening campaign may have been political in motivation, it also typified his pessimistic outlook. Essex frequently displayed considerable personal courage, and was popular with his troops, who knew him as "Old Robin", but he proved unable to put the good of his cause above personal grudges. His strategic insight was patchy, as he consistently allowed his opponents to get between him and his base, though his successful relief of Gloucester in 1643 has been held to have been the turning point of the First Civil War.

S.r William Waller Major Gen:
of Surry Sussex & Hampshire

Sir William Waller (1598–1668)

Waller, like his friend Ralph Hopton, gained his first military experience on the Continent. Joining Parliament on the outbreak of wear, Waller earned an initial reputation in fighting along the Welsh Border, and then engaged Hopton in a closely-fought duel in the West Country, until defeated at Roundway Down. He gained his revenge at Cheriton, but was defeated again at Cropredy Bridge. His atrocious personal relationship with Essex did much to lose the Parliamentarians the 1644 Campaign in the South. Though described by one opponent as the "best shifter and chooser of ground when he was not Master of the Field that I ever saw", Waller was a poor disciplinarian, and tended to err too much on the side of caution.

The most Noble Ferdinand
Lord Fairfax Generall of the
Northern Countyes

Ferdinando, 2nd Lord Fairfax (1584-1648)

Fairfax served a brief military apprenticeship in the Low Countries earning the verdict that "he makes a tolerable country justice, but is a mere coward at fighting". As a leading local opponent of the King in Yorkshire , however, Fairfax was appointed to command the Parliamentarian forces there on the outbreak of war. Greatly outnumbered by his opponents, Fairfax was quickly forced onto the strategic defensive, which in any case suited his style of fighting.

Fairfax had a fairly dismal war, making a quick departure from the field of Adwalton Moor , and also quitting the action at Marston Moor with some alacrity. However, he defended Hull with some tenacity, and Fairfax's support was probably vital for the survival of Parliament's cause in the North.

The most Excellent Sᵣ Thomas Fairfax
Captin Generall of the Armyes etc :

Thomas, 3rd Lord Fairfax (1612-1671)

Son of Ferdinando, Sir Thomas served in the Low Countries, and later in the 1st Scots War. During the opening years of the First Civil War, he acted as his father's second-in-command, and the moving spirit of Parliament's operations in the North.

Fairfax was an excellent fighting soldier, especially in tight corners. His attitude on such occasions was typified by his comment as he led an attack at the battle of Winceby - "Come, let us fall on, I have never prospered better than when I fought against the enemy three or four to one". Though, as a general, Fairfax's record was somewhat chequered, as a commander "Black Tom" was beloved of his soldiers. In 1645, he was to prove an excellent commander-in-chief of the New Model Army, and did much to ensure its victory in the closing campaigns of the First Civil War.

During the Second Civil War, Fairfax broke the Royalist insurrections in South East England, but he grew increasingly out of sympathy with political developments, and gradually withdrew from public life. Fairfax may be rated as the most effective of the Parliamentarian commanders in the First Civil War.

The Religious successfull and truly Valliant
Lieutenant Generall Cromwell

Oliver Cromwell (1599-1658)

Cromwell, despite his prominence in later eyes, had no military experience prior to the outbreak of war, and owed his initial appointment to political considerations. But he quickly proved to be a capable soldier, early seeing the importance of discipline and motivation. His ideal was "a plain russet-coated captain that knows what he fights for, and loves what he knows".

Cromwell began to gain his reputation as a commander of horse in a series of actions in East Anglia in the summer and autumn of 1643, and his leading role in the victory at Marston Moor served both to confirm Cromwell's growing ability, and to confirm his appointment as second-in-command of the New Model Army.

Cromwell's military importance during the First Civil War has been greatly exaggerated by posterity; his true claims to military greatness lie in his operations during later years, notably his triumph at Preston in 1648, and his victories at Dunbar and Worcester.

His Exellence Alexander Lasley
Generall of the Scotch Army

Alexander Leslie, Earl of Leven (1580–1661)

An "old, little, crooked soldier", Leven was an illiterate, illegitimate soldier of fortune who served on the continent and with Gustavus Adolphus of Sweden for over 30 years. He commanded the Covenanting Army in 1639 and 1640, and in 1644 was general of the Scottish Army which invaded England. He proved to be a cautious commander on this occasion, partly because he was aware of the limitations of the material under his command. Commander-in-Chief at Marston Moor, Leven was also the first of the generals to quit the field, earning the comment from his fellow Scottish professional, Sir James Turner, who had a long-standing feud with Leven; "There was reason he should take the start... because he had the furthest home". Henceforward, distracted by Montrose's activities at home, and disagreements with Parliament, the Scottish Army played a somewhat inactive role in the war. Leven had been a competent soldier, but by the outbreak of the Civil War he had grown over-cautious, and was probably too old for active command.

The Officers

Although the term "officers" theoretically included all those holding an office, including drummers and clerks, in practice it may be held to mean commissioned officers and N.C.O.s. In a foot company the officers comprised a Captain, who commanded the whole unit, plus half the musketeers, his second-in-command, a Lieutenant, who also commanded the remaining musketeers, and an Ensign , who carried the colours and also commanded the pikemen. There would also have been three sergeants, three corporals and three drummers.

The field officers of a regiment of foot consisted of the Colonel, Lieutenant-Colonel and Sergeant- Major (already beginning to be abbreviated to Major). All three were also theoretically Captains of their own companies.

Organisation of cavalry was similar. Here the basic unit was the Troop, with four commissioned officers, three corporals, two trumpeters, and perhaps occasionally a farrier and even a surgeon.

A Captain was once again in command, with a Lieutenant and a Cornet corresponding to the Ensign in a company of Foot. Finally there was the Quartermaster, who as suggested by his title, was responsible for quartering the troop, though he also had the normal responsibilities of an officer, ranking as fourth in command.

Obviously all armies endeavoured to secure as high a proportion of experienced officers as possible; the Scots indeed attempted to formalise the system with professionals occupying designated ranks. This was never the case with the English armies, though from the start of the conflict, large numbers of company commanders were professional soldiers, and the remainder, if they lived long enough, quickly learnt.

Professional soldiers were of course, traditionally prone to flexible loyalties, changing sides easily. Strangely enough, this seems to have been accepted practice so far as the large number of Scottish professionals were concerned (the record was probably held by Sir John Urry, who switched allegiances three times), but English soldiers found it to be a much riskier business.

The popular image of the aristocratic Royalist officer corps, contrasted with their Godly more humble Parliamentarian counterparts, is not borne out by the reality. Both sides had a high proportion of nobility in senior command, whilst the bulk of officers lower down the line on both sides were gentlemen with Trained Band experience. Nonetheless, there were officers in both armies from a surprising variety of civilian backgrounds, from cobblers to choristers to play actors. Many of them proved surprisingly effective in their new military careers.

Fig: 7.
Par: 4.
Cap: 6.

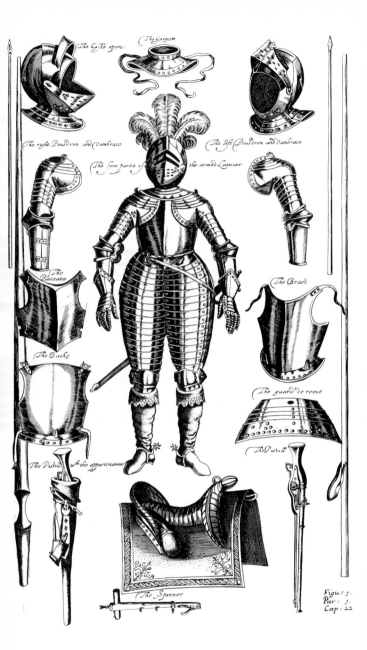

The Caske opon

The Gorgett

The righe Pouldron and Vambrace

The loft Pouldron and Vambrace

The fore parte of the armed Lancier

The Placcate

The Breast

The Backe

The guard de reine

The Pistoll with the appurtenances

The Pistoll

The Spanner

Figu: 3.
Par: 3.
Cap: 22.

The Horse

The horse were traditionally regarded as the elite battle-winning arm, and ideally, the military theorists of the time held that an army should consist of one horseman to every two footmen. Needless to say, these proportions were not strictly adhered to; for reasons examined below the Royalist armies, for example, tended to have a much higher proportion of horse to foot as the war went on.

Three types of cavalry were recognised by military writers. First were the heavy cavalry, or cuirassiers, in three quarter armour over buff coats, armed with sword and pair of pistols and riding a horse of 15 hands. Although Parliament raised one complete Regiment of Cuirassiers - Sir Arthur Haselrig's "Lobsters"- the fully - equipped cuirassier was a fairly rare sight on Civil War battlefields. This was partly because of the difficulty encountered in obtaining suitable mounts and equipment, and also because their heavy armour was so uncomfortable. "It will kill a man", wrote Sir Edmund Verney in 1638, "to serve in a whole cuirass."

Also rarely if ever seen, other than in the Scottish Army, where they were widely employed with some success, were the other species of heavy cavalry, the lancers.

The standard cavalryman employed by all sides in the war was the harquebusier. Theoretically classed as a "light" horseman, the harquebusier wore ideally a buff

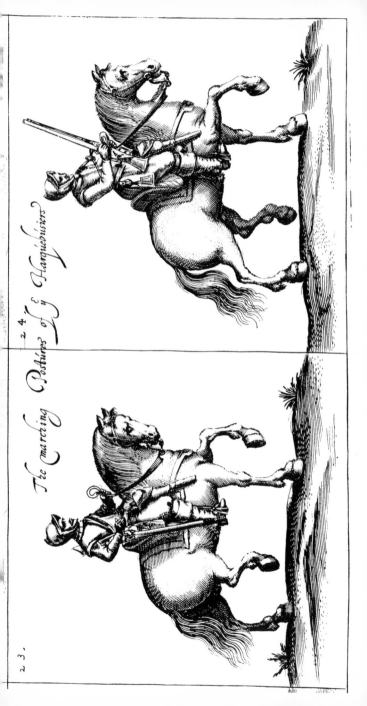

The marching Postures of y Harquebusiers

coat, back and breast and pot helmet, and was armed with sword, pair of pistols and carbine. In practice, particularly in the Royalist armies in the early stages of the war, this theoretical standard of perfection was rarely achieved.

The Earl of Clarendon described the King's horse at the battle of Edgehill in October 1642; "Amongst the horse, the officers had their full desire if they were able to procure old backs and breasts and pots with pistols and carbines for their two or three first ranks, and swords for the rest; themselves (and some soldiers by their examples) having gotten besides their pistols and swords a short poleaxe."

In these opening operations, it may well be that the Parliamentarian horse, with the resources of the armouries of the Tower and Hull at their disposal, and initially easier access to foreign imports, were better equipped, but any difference between the outfitting of the horse of the two sides quickly disappeared. By late 1643, the average Royalist trooper would have been equipped with lobster-tailed helmet, back and breast, and possibly a fairly cheap and nasty buff coat, and armed with sword, and pistols or carbine. His Parliamentarian opponent would have been equipped in exactly the same way, and the only way in which the horse of each side could be differentiated was by the colour of the sash which they wore- crimson for the Royalists, and orange for the Parliamentarians, at least in the Earl of Essex's army.

In both armies the theoretical strength of a regiment of horse was about 500 men, though actual totals varied enormously, and in practice regiments were brigaded together to form viable fighting formations.

It is worth examining the types of recruits who fought in the cavalry units of both sides. Once again, the popular image is of roistering, extravagantly dressed Cavaliers versus soberly clad, psalm-singing Roundheads, and once more, the reality was rather different. It should be remembered that in 17th century England the great majority of the male population would be able to ride at least adequately, giving great scope for cavalry recruitment. It is probably true that the Royalist horse may have contained a marginally higher proportion of gentry and aristocracy than their opponents, but the majority of troopers on both sides were drawn from similar social origins. Commonly, they were tradesmen, husbandmen, better-off agricultural workers and gentlemens' servants, but they would also have included a large number of urban tradesmen.

Also frequently employed were foreign volunteers and mercenaries, on the Royalist side frequently French, and Dutch and Germans were common to both. Perhaps the most remarkable recruit to serve in any of the armies was a certain Captain Frances Dalyell, the Scottish illegitimate daughter of the Earl of Carnwath, who led a troop in the Northern Royalist forces!

So, though it is clear that the horse of King and Parliament differed little in basic organisation, how can the initial striking superiority of the Royalist horse be explained? The reason seems to lie in the perceived role of harquebusiers, and the way in which they were actually employed by Prince Rupert and his commanders.

Harquebusiers were generally classed as "light" cavalry, with the role of guarding flanks and taking the initial brunt of any fighting until the cuirassiers were committed in a battle-winning crushing charge. Parliament initially followed the rule-book, and employed their horse in this way. Thus, in the early battles of the war, we tend to see

the Parliamentarian horse standing still to meet enemy attack, and relying on their pistols and carbines to blunt the impact of the Royalist assault.

There were always a number of problems with this approach; to be effective it needed well-trained troops, adept with their weaponry, and with good morale. The early Parliamentarian horse generally lacked all of these attributes. More important was Rupert's decision to employ his horse as though they actually were cuirassiers! The tactics adopted by the horse of the Oxford Army from as early as the battle of Edgehill is described by an officer who took part, Richard Bulstrode. After forming his men into three ranks (five or six was the formation normally recommended for harquebusiers) Prince Rupert rode along the ranks giving "Positive Orders to the Horse to march as Close as possible, keeping their Ranks with Sword in Hand, to receive the Enemy's Shot without firing either Carbin or Pistol, till we broke in amongst the Enemy and then to make use of our Fire-arms as need should require."

These were the classic tactics of the cuirassier - significant is the absence of the word "charge" in the description - contrary to popular belief, a full-blooded charge was an extremely rare occurance, as it would serve mainly to disrupt the close formation vital for an effective attack. The normal speed is usually described as a "full trot".

The result of Rupert's tactics at Edgehill were devastatingly successful; all of the Parliamentarian horse hit by his attack were routed, and this set the pattern for the next year. A Royalist captain, Richard Atkyns, gives a graphic description of what it was like to take part in such a cavalry action, in this case the great Royalist victory at Roundway Down (July 13, 1643).

"Twas my fortune in a direct line to charge their general of horse (Sir Arthur Haselrigge), which I supposed to be so by his place; he discharged his carbine first, but at a distance not to hurt us, and afterwards one of his pistols, before I came up to him, and missed with both; I then immediately struck into him, and touched him before I discharged mine; and I'm sure I hit him, for he staggered, and presently wheeled off from his party and ran. (I followed him) and in six score yards I came up to him, and discharged the other pistol at him, and I'm sure I hit his head, for I touched it before I gave fire, and it amazed him at that present, but he was too well armed all over for a pistol bullet to do him any hurt, having a coat of mail over his arms and a headpiece (I am confident) musket proof, (Sir Arthur and his Regiment of "Lobsters" were equipped as cuirassiers) his sword had two edges and a ridge in the middle, and mine a strong tuck (the heavy, straight-bladed weapon commonly used by cuirassiers); after I had slackened my pace a little, he was gone twenty yards from me, riding three quarters speed, and down the side of a hill, his posture was waving his sword on the right anmd left hand of his horse, not looking back whether he was pursued or not, (as I conceive) to daunt any horse that should come up to him; about six score more I came up with him again (having a very swift horse that Cornet Washnage gave me) and stuck by him a good while, and tried him from head to the saddle, and could not penetrate him, nor do him any hurt,; but in this attempt he cut my horses's nose, that you might put your finger in the wound, and gave me such a blow on the inside of my arm amongst the veins that I could hardly hold my sword; he went on as before, I slackened my pace again, and found my horse drop blood, and not so bold as before; but about eight score more (paces) I came up to him again, thinking to have pulled him off his horse; but he now having found the way, struck my horse upon the cheek, and cut off half the headstall of my bridle, but falling off from him, I ran his horse into the body and resolved to attempt nothing further than to kill his horse; all this time we were together hand to fist.

In this nick of time came up Mr Holmes to my assistance, (who never failed me in time of danger) and went up to him with great resolution, and felt him before he discharged his pistol, and though I saw him hit him, 'twas but a flea-biting to him; whilst he charged him, I employed myself in killing his horse, and ran him into several places, and upon the faltering of his horse his head-piece opened behind, and I gave him a prick in the neck, and I had run him through the head if my horse had not stumbled at the same place; then came in Captain Buck a gentleman of my troop, and discharged his pistol upon him also, but with the same success as before, and being a very strong man, and charging with a mighty hanger, stormed him and amazed him, but fell off again; by this time his horse began to be faint with bleeding, and fell off his rate, at which said Sir Arthur, "What good will it do you to kill a poor man?" Said I, "Take Quarter then", with that he stopped his horse, and I came up to him, and bid him deliver his sword, which he was loathe to do; and being tied twice about his wrist, he was fumbling a great while before he would part with it; but before he delivered it, there was a runaway troop of theirs that had espied him in hold; says one of them "My Lord General is taken prisoner"; says another, "Sir Arthur Haselrigge is taken

prisoner, face about and charge", with that they rallied and charged us, and rescued him; wherein I received a shot with a pistol, which only took off the skin upon the blade bone of my shoulder".

Not all opponents proved as tough nuts to crack as the redoubtable Sir Arthur, but by the autumn of 1643 the superiority of the Royalist horse began to be eroded, as more and more of the Parliamentarian commanders began to adopt the same tactics.

One of the first to see the value of Rupert's tactics was Cromwell, and by October 1643, at the Battle of Winceby, he was employing very similar methods. "Colonel Cromwell fell with brave resolution upon the enemy.... Truely this first charge was so home given, and performed with such admirable courage and resolution by our troops, that the enemy stood not another, but were driven back upon their own body which was to have seconded them, and at last put these into a plain disorder; and thus in less than half an hour's fight they were all quite routed."

The final factor which in the end established the superiority of the Parliamentarian horse was discipline. By 1644, the majority of the better units of horse on both sides were probably adopting the tactics of cuirassiers, but the Royalists had one major failing, described by the Earl of Clarendon; "Though the King's troops, prevailed in the charge and routed those they charged, they seldom rallied themselves again in order, nor could be brought to make a second charge the same day.... whereas the other troops, if they prevailed, or though they were beaten and routed, presently rallied again, and stood in good order till they received new orders." Rupert's men first displayed this weakness at Edgehill, and were still doing so at Naseby in

1645, whilst Cromwell's ability to control his men and keep a reserve in hand after defeating his immediate opponents, played a major part in the Parliamentarian victories at Marston Moor and Naseby.

The reasons for this Royalist failure are perhaps debatable; undoubtedly the brigading together of numerous fragmented units, and at Naseby at least, the presence of a large number of "second-line troops" who had not previously served with the Oxford Army, were contributing factors.

Whatever the cause, by 1645 the Parliamentarian horse, particularly those serving with the New Model Army, had established a moral and tactical superiority over their opponents which was never again to be seriously challenged.

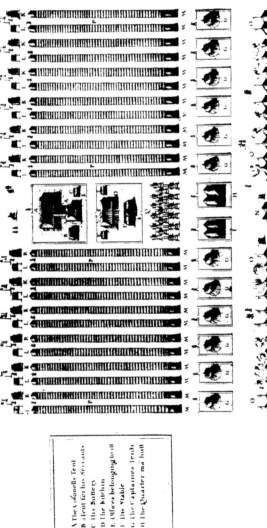

A The Colonells Tent
B Tent for his Servants
C His Buttery
D The kitchin
E Offices belonging to it
F Its Stable
G The Captaines Tents
H The Quarter ma hutt

I The Minist's Surgeons
K The Levetennants hutt
L The Ensignes hutte
M The Serjeants hutte
N The Martialls hutt
O The Suttlers hutts
P Streetes through ye
Q The place for the woggo

THE DISPOSITION OF A SINGLE REGIMENT OF INFANTRY IN THE FIELDS
ACCORDING TO THE PRESENT DISCIPLINE OF HIS MAJESTY KING CHARLES'

The Foot

The middle and late 17th century saw a steady increase in the importance and effectiveness of infantry; by 1637, the Scottish professional soldier, Robert Monro was writing, "My choice shall ever be to command on foot." This greater importance was caused by improved firearms and better drill and tactics, but the outbreak of the Civil War found the foot still in a state of transition.

A Regiment of Foot theoretically totalled 1,200 men, in 10 companies; with a recommended ratio of one pikeman to two musketeers. This ratio in practice varied widely, as indeed did opinions as to the most desirable proportions. The Scottish professional soldier, Sir James Turner, expressed the dilemma in picturesque terms.

"In process of time when soldiers became expert at the Musquet, companies both strong and weak soever were divided into three parts, two thirds whereof were pikemen, and one third musqueteers; thereafter the Musquet craved half the game and got it. But equality for the most part is short lived, and so fared it in this, for very soon the musqueteers challenged the two thirds, and obtained them, leaving but one third for the pikemen, which for the most part they keep, though in several places.... pikes are sent to look for their fortunes elsewhere."

Pikemen

The pike was traditionally regarded as the more honourable weapon of the foot soldier, partly because of its antiquity, and also because in theory at least, pikemen had to be taller and stronger than musketeers. It must be said, however, that those bearing this weapon frequently showed little appreciation of its honourable qualities. In theory, a pike should have been between 16 and 18 feet in length, but in the field, soldiers frequently shortened it to about 12 feet, both for greater ease of carrying and also as a convenient source of firewood! Pikemen also carried a poor quality sword, which was used mainly for brawling, terrorising civilians and chopping firewood, though it must have had its uses in battle as well.

Pikemen are traditionally pictured as wearing armour, consisting of back and breastplates, tassets protecting the thighs, a gorget at the throat and an iron headpiece. In fact, the evidence indicates that the amount of armour worn decreased rapidly, and indeed there is nothing to suggest that it was ever widely worn on either side. Clarendon remarks in his description of the Royalist foot at Edgehill, "in the whole body there was not one pikeman had a corselet (armour)", and there is no evidence to suggest that this situation was ever remedied, or that there was ever thought to be any need to do so.

In battle, the role of the pikeman was somewhat limited. Pikes had to be employed in mass formation, and, when fighting those of their own kind, the tactic was to engage in what was known as "push of pike". The result was basically a somewhat disorganised jostling and scrambling, much like a modern rugby scrum, in which the contending pikemen, far from attempting to impale their opponents on their pikes, tried to push them off balance or off their feet. Such an encounter occurred at Stratton in May 1643; "The fight continued doubtful with many countenances of various events till about three of the clock in the afternoone, by which tyme the ammunicion belonging to the Cornish army was almost spent. It fortuned that on the Avenew where Sir Bevile Grenvile advanc'd in the head of his Pikes in the way, and Sir Jo. Berkeley ledd the muskettiers on each syde of him, Major General Chudleigh with a stand of pikes charged Sir Beville Grenvile so smartlie, that there was some disorder, Sir Bevile Grenvile in person overthrown..."

Often, if one or both sides lacked enthusiasm, all that might happen when the opposing pikes met would be an ineffective fencing action which did little or no damage. There was frequently indeed, a reluctance among both pike and musketeers to become seriously engaged for long; The future James II wrote of events which he witnesssed at Edgehill ... "the foot thus engaged in such warm and close service, it were reasonable to suppose that one side should run and be disordered; but it happened otherwise, for each as if by mutual consent retired some few paces, and then struck down their colours, continuing to fire at each other even until night, a thing so extraordinary as nothing less than so many witnesses as were present could make it credible." It would become a much more believable occurrence as the war went on.

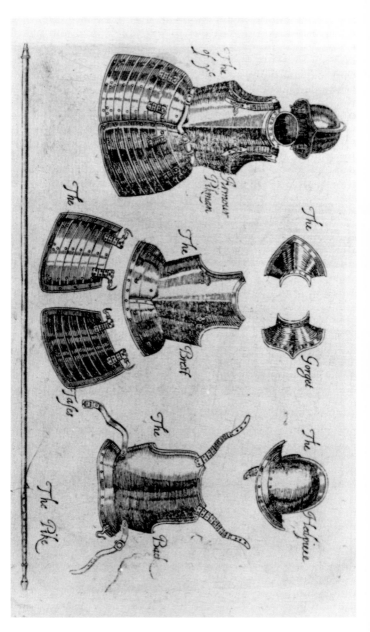

Musketeers

Musketeers not only made up at least two thirds of the strength of the ideal foot regiment, they also bore an increasingly large share of the fighting.

The standard firearm of the Civil War musketeer was the matchlock, a weapon considerably more effective than sometimes suggested. In perfect conditions, a shot from a matchlock could killed an unarmoured man at 600 yards, though its effective range was normally regarded as much less; the veterans of the Spanish Army of Flanders, for example, would only begin to open fire in earnest at ranges as close as 20 yards.

The matchlock had the advantages of simplicity of construction and relative cheapness; it had the disadvantage of being unreliable in wet or windy weather, when its powder might become damp or the length of match cord used to fire it be extinguished. The earlier models, which were 4 feet in length, were fairly heavy, and in theory required a musket rest to be fired from. Shorter and lighter weapons were already in the course of introduction, and the rest seems gradually to have been abandoned.

Much misunderstanding has occurred regarding the rate at which matchlocks could be fired. There were complicated and lengthy procedures laid down in the various drill manuals of the period, but these were replaced in the field by much simpler methods which boiled down to

The armes of ye Musketier

three commands; MAKE READY - PRESENT - FIRE!, and allowed the matchlock to be discharged every thirty seconds rather than in as long a period as five minutes, as is sometimes suggested.

Musketeers were also armed with the same poor-quality sword as the pikemen, and employed it for similar purposes, preferring, if engaged in hand-to-hand fighting , to use the butt-ends of their muskets.

Various methods were employed to carry ammunition; the bandolier was the most popular, carrying (usually) 12 tin or wooden powder chargers. Also used, particularly in the Royalist forces, were powder bags, carried at the waist by a belt or girdle. In other cases, cartridges might simply be stuffed in the soldiers' pockets.

Also sometimes issued were firelocks or flintlocks, more complicated but theoretically more reliable weapons, which were mainly issued to troops guarding ammunition and to various special service units.

Various tactical formations were adopted to maximise the effectiveness of the matchlock. Regiments were normally deployed in six ranks, each rank firing in succession, the first theoretically being re-loaded and ready for action by the time the others had given fire. Another tactic was to combine the musketeers into three ranks, one kneeling, one stooping and the rear one standing, and to fire a simultaneous volley, known as a "salvee". this might be devastating, but was a risky business as there might be no time to reload before the enemy was on the firers. It seems to have been a tactic popular with the Royalists preceding a violent charge.

One problem, perennial in warfare in general, but common among untrained and unmotivated soldiers of

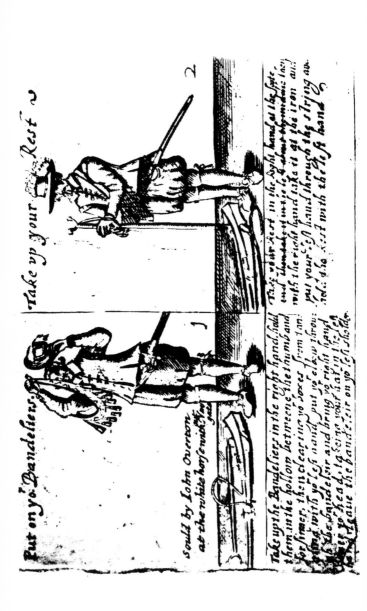

the Civil War armies, was the habit of simply firing as quickly as possible, with little regard to drill, and then heading for the rear. One result of this was a tendency to shoot the men in the rank ahead in the back! Another was a habit of firing wildly into the air; this was noted in 1648 at the battle of Preston by Captain Johyn Hodgson, who wrote of some newly levied Royalist foot, "the enemy let fly at us. They shot at the skies, which did so encourage our men that they were willing to venture upon any attempt." Also common was a natural inclination to take up position under cover and then do as little as possible. This seems to have happened with many of the Royalist foot at the First Battle of Newbury, where they were said to have "played the poltroon extremely".

Whilst massed volleys at close range could be effective, it was quite common for one side to break fairly quickly, the bulk of casualties usually being inflicted by cavalry in the course of the pursuit.

There is no doubt that disciplined musketeers could be highly effective. An excellent example of this occurs in Montrose's victories in Scotland. Popular legend still credits his successes to the exploits of his Highlanders and the claimed fury of their "Highland Charge". The reality was rather different; a description by General Hawley of the Jacobite forces of 1745 is an accurate summary of Montrose's Highlanders as well. "They commonly form their front rank of what they call their best men or True Highlanders the number of which being always but few, when they form in battalions they commonly form four deep, and these Highlanders form the front of the four, the rest being lowlanders and arrant scum." Most of the Highlanders were generally ill-armed and worse disci-

plined, and their "charge", whilst on occasion terrifying to ill-disciplined or raw troops, was more sound and fury than hard military threat, unless the enemy panicked and broke, when the resulting slaughter would be terrible.

Montrose actually relied on the well-trained musketeers of his three regiments of Irish mercenaries, mostly professional soldiers, and the regular units raised in North -East Scotland. These, together later with the regiment of regular cavalry brought over by Lord Gordon, provided the muscle which enabled Montrose to defeat successive Government forces and invade the Lowlands. Without them, as events after Philliphaugh were to prove, he presented no serious threat at all.

Well-handled and motivated foot could be very effective; one of the hardest-fought actions of the war occurred at the First Battle of Newbury (October 20, 1643) when a brigade of Royalist horse led by Sir John Byron was ordered to support the Royalist foot in clearing a well-held Parliamentarian position on Round Hill. After a preliminary reconnaissance, during which the King's Secretary of State, Lord Falkland, was killed when he tried to ride through a narrow gap in a hedge, and Byron's own horse was killed by a shot in the throat, "The passage being made somewhat wide, and I not having another horse, drew in my own troop first, giving orders for the rest to follow and charged the enemy, who entertained us with a great salvo of musket shot, and discharged their two drakes upon us laden with case shot, which killed some and hurt many of my men, so that we were forced to wheel off and could not meet them at that charge". The Parliamentarians fell back to the next field, or "close", taking their two guns with them. Byron sent in another of his regiments, commanded by Sir Thomas Aston, "which beat them to the end of the close, where they faced us again, having the advantage of a hedge at their backs and poured in another volley of shot upon us, when Sir Thomas Aston's horse was killed under him, and withall kept us off with their pikes. " The Parliamentarians made another retreat, and were charged for a third time by the Royalist horse, but managed to withdraw substantially intact, having inflicted 100 casualties - a 1/4 of its strength - on Byron's Regiment alone.

A contrasting incident, illustrating the ineffectiveness of poorly motivated foot, occurred during the Lostwithiel Campaign of 1644. In the fighting on August 31st, the King's Lifeguard of horse were sent to engage some of the Earl of Essex's foot who were attempting a stand; "about 11 of the clocke Captain Brett led up the Queen's troope, and most gallantly in view of the King charged their foote and beate them from their hedge, killing many of them, notwithstanding that their musquets made abundance of shott at his men: he received a shott in the left arm in the first field, and one of his men, La Plunne, a Frenchman killed, yet most gallantly went on and brought his men off; his cornett's horse shott, with 2 other horses, and 2 more wounded: he retreated to be dresst, and the King called him and tooke his sword which was drawne in his hand, and knighted Sir Edward Brett on his horse's back."

As the war progressed, there was a tendency to increase the proportion of musketeers among the foot. This was carried to its ultimate point in the Royalist armies, where, once the initial shortage of firearms had been overcome by foreign imports and increased production, a number of regiments were re-equipped entirely as musketeers. This helped overcome the problems resulting from understrength units and also provided greatly increased mobility – unlike pikemen, musketeers could be mounted if need be, and still retain their effectiveness.

March with your rest in your hand.

Dragoons

These troops, basically mounted infantry, had a rather chequered Civil War career. At the beginning of hostilities, both sides raised dragoons in large numbers. In theory, dragoons might be armed with both pikes and muskets, but for obvious practical reasons, it seems unlikely that any employed in the Civil War were equipped with pikes. The normal equipment was "a good fire and cock musket, something a wider bore than ordinary, hanging in a belt by a sweble [swivel] at his side, with a good sword and ordinary horse."

Sir James Turner described the uses of dragoons; "Dragoons then go not only before to guard Passes (as some imagine) but to fight in open Field: for if an Enemy rencounter with a Cavalry in a champaign or open Heath, the Dragoons are obliged to alight, and mix themselves with the Squads of Horse, as they shall be commanded; and their continuate Firing, before the Horse come to the charge, will no doubt, be very hurtful to the Enemy: If the encounter be in a closed Countrey, they serve well to line Hedges, and possess Enclosures..."

The main value of dragoons lay in their mobility, and for use in guarding flanks, raiding, skirmishing and clearing outlying enemy defenders. They generally dwindled in numbers as the war went on. This was partly because the limited suppliers of horses available were more urgently needed by the cavalry, and, because of their normal tactic of dismounting to fight, dragoons were frequently unable to recover their horses if defeated.

Separate dragoon regiments had largely disappeared from the Royalist army by 1644, though some individual troops remained attached to regiments of horse. They were replaced by detachments of musketeers mounted for specific operations. The Scots made good use of dragoons; Fraser's Regiment distinguished itself at Marston Moor.

The New Model Army included a dragoon regiment commanded by Colonel John Okey, which played an important role in the battle. Sent to line the hedges on the flank of the Royalist advance, Okey and his men quickly found themselves in a tight spot. "By that time" wrote Okey " I could get my men to light and deliver up their horses in a little close, the enemy drew towards us, which my men perceiving, they with shooting and rejoycing received them, although they were encompassed on the one side with the king's horse and on the other side with foot and horse [trying] to get the close; but it pleased God that we beat off both the horse and the foot... and kept our ground." Later the Parliamentarians counterattacked "Which I perceiving, caused all my men to mount and charge into their foot, which accordingly they did, and took all their colours and 500 prisoners." It was a good example of the versatility of well-led dragoons.

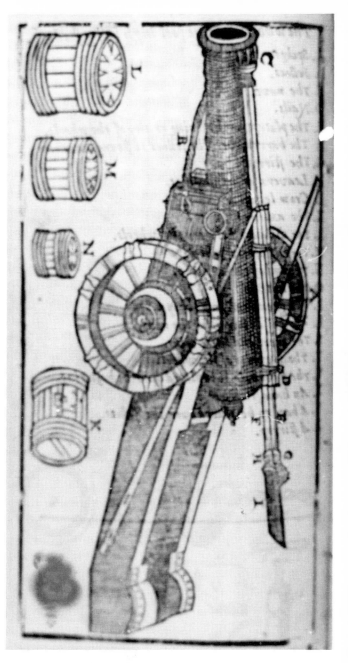

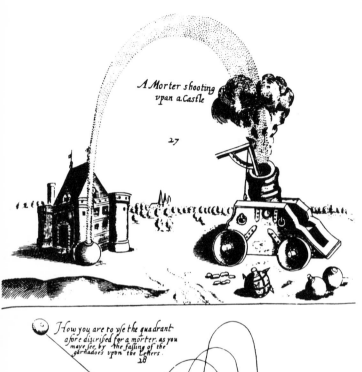

A Morter shooting vpan a Casfle

27

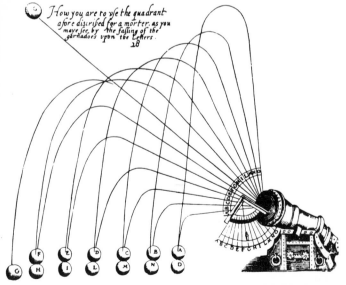

How you are to vse the quadrant afore discribed for a morter. as you maye see. by the falling of the garnadoes vpon the Letters.

28

Artillery

Artillery was less generally used in the Civil Wars than was the case on the Continent. Its main value was felt to be in siege warfare, and its effects in battle were fairly small.

There were various methods of classifying the different types of guns in use, with their colourful array of names, ranging from the massive full cannon firing a shot of 63 lb, through culverins, demi-culverins, sakers minions, falconets and drakes - the latter being a 3pdr or less. In practice the real division was between siege artillery, the cannon royal, full cannon, culverin and mortar, and the field artillery, demi-culverin downwards.

As with the musket, much has often been made of the slow rate of fire and inaccuracy of Civil War artillery, but this again is in part based upon the assumption that the cumbersome procedures of the drill book were actually followed in the field. One of the main practical problems encountered in employing artillery was its cumbersomeness and difficulty in transporting it. This was particularly the case with siege artillery. The New Model Army's siege train frequently met with problems, and the preferred solution wherever possible was to ship such massive guns by water, a procedure not without its dangers; in 1648 Cromwell's siege of Pembroke Castle was delayed when his guns were lost in the Severn Estuary.

Even the train of artillery which normally accompanied a field army consumed many horses and additional transport. Below is the inventory among the Royalist Ordnance Papers for a proposed Train of Artillery in May 1643;

2	Demi-Cannons	38	horses
2	Culverins	26	horses
2	12 pdrs	22	horses
1	Demi-culverin	5	horses
4	6-pdrs	20	horses
1	Saker	5	horses
5	3pdrs	15	horses
2	Rabonetts	6	horses
1	Mortar	7	horses

Transport for ammunition, and all the other necessary items of equipment would require 51 carts and 399 horses.

The artillery, together with other matters relating to arms and ammunition, was normally under the control of A General of the Ordnance. In the Royalist Army, this command was exercised for much of the war by Lord Henry Percy, generally regarded as ineffective, though he had a highly capable deputy in Sir John Heydon. Further down in the hierarchy were Master Gunners (again usually professional soldiers) Gentlemen of the Ordnance, Engineers, and the gun crews themselves - gunners, matrosses and pioneers, together with the host of carters and drivers required. An artillery train would also contain various other specialists necessary to maintain its efficiency. Among them were smiths, carpenters, wheelwrights, farriers, coopers, harness makers, ladle makers and tent makers.

A demi-cannon would be crewed by 3 gunners and 6 matrosses, whilst the middle calibre pieces averaged 2 gunners and 4 matrosses.

Firing artillery was generally reckoned a hazardous business; accidents with powder, and guns blowing up or discharging prematurely were common occurrences. Partly because of this, and the mathematical expertise necessary to employ the artillery effectively, gunners were held in considerable esteem.

Though there are many accounts of the use of artillery in sieges, where, employed properly in the right circumstances it could be decisive, little mention is normally made of its use in the field. This is partly perhaps because no account of any major action written by an artillery officer has survived. Yet the evidence suggests that on some occasions, at least, guns were heavily used, sometimes with notable effect. The battle of Edgehill opened with an an artillery exchange , the rival guns exchanged fire prior to the action being joined at Marston Moor, and, most significantly, the First Battle of Newbury saw the most sustained artillery exchanges of any battle in the war, with heavy losses being inflicted, especially upon the London Trained Bands. One factor telling against the frequent extensive use of artillery was probably the vast expenditure of powder which it incurred.

It was common practice to attach a couple of light guns to each brigade of foot, and in the Scottish Army this was carried considerably further with the adoption of light, easily transported leather or "frame" guns, which were employed in large numbers at Marston Moor, though with what results is unclear.

Coats and Colours

From the beginning of hostilities both sides recognised the desirability of providing uniform dress for their troops, but the reality proved to be highly confusing. During the early campaigns there were a wide variety of coat colours among individual regiments, blue, red, orange, green, white, and possibly even purple being among the examples known in the foot regiments. Gradually however a greater degree of uniformity crept in. From the summer of 1643 there was an attempt made to dress the Foot regiments of the Oxford Army in either blue or red, though reinforcements and detachments from elsewhere could still add a variety of hue. Best known, of course, is the New Model Army, "the men are redcoats all, the whole army only are distinguished by several facings of their coats". But even this standardisation appears to have been a gradual process, and with issues of new clothing only normally taking place once a year, the average Civil War army must usually have displayed a distinctly motley appearance. In some cases choice of coat colour was dictated by local considerations - the Earl of Newcastle's Northern Royalists included a number of whitecoat regiments - actually probably a sort of greyish brown- because of the ready availability of undyed woollen cloth in that region. They also frequently wore blue bonnets of a Scottish variety. The Scots themselves seem to have achieved a considerable degree of uniformity

Colonel.

5. Captain.

1 Captain.

10 Files of Pikes. | 10 Files of Pikes. | 10 Files of Pikes. | 10 Files of Pikes. | 10 Files of Pikes.

Lieut. Colonel.

Colonel.

The 2 Captain.

The 4 Cap. Eldest Captain.

The 2 Cap. Lieutenant.

The Lieut. Col. Lieutenant.

This Squad. contains 24 files Musket.

Majors Lieu.

This Squad. contains 24 files Musket.

The 3 Cap.

This Squad. contains 24 files Musket.

This Squad. contains 24 files Pikes.

This Squadron contains 24 files of Pikes.

This Squad. contains 24 files Musket.

The 2 Cap. Lieut. place.

The 3 Cap. Lieutenant.

The 1 Cap. Lieutenant.

The Cap. Lieutena. bringer-up

The 4 Cap. Lieutenant.

from the beginning, issuing their men with suits of "hodden grey", and the ubiquitous blue bonnet.

Officers tended to wear what they chose, and there is no evidence to suggest much uniformity of dress amongst the horse.

Very often, in reality, troops wore various items of civilian clothing, either their own, looted, or "donated" by more or less willing citizens. In these circumstances confusion in battle was frequent, not always clarified by the use of field signs such as scraps of white paper, arm bands or sprigs of plants.

It was partly to overcome this problem, as well as to provide rallying points and a certain espirit de corps, that flags were used. Here again a number of misconceptions frequently arise. It is often said that the base colour of an infantry flag would be the same as the coat colour of the regiment concerned; in practice this was seldom the case. In theory each company of foot carried its own flag, normally made of painted taffeta or silk, and measuring about $6^1/2$ foot square. A system was normally employed identifying each company by the number of regimental symbols carried on it flag. A commonly employed system was one described by Thomas Venn; "the Colonel's Colours in the first place is of a pure and clean colour, without any mixture. The Lieutenant-Colonel's colour only with St. George's Armes in the upper corner next the staff, the Major's the same, but in the lower and outermost corner with a little stream blazant, and every Captain with St George's Armes alone, but with so many spots or several devices as pertain to the dignity of their respective places." Thus a First Captain would have one symbol, a ball, cross or other device, on his flag, a Second Captain two, and so on.

Scots colours were considerably different in their design, and the saltire, or St. Andrew's Cross, was prominently employed.

Once again, there is good reason to believe that the actual situation on the Civil War battlefield was a good deal less tidy than the theory outlined above. Regiments were frequently amalgamated, and the colours of all the original units might continue to be flown by the new formation. There is also ample evidence to suggest that a Regiment might radically change the style and design of its colours several times during its career, sometimes dictated by such basic considerations as what designs the flagmaker actually had in stock in sufficient quantities at the time that an order was placed!

Finally, quite a number of regiments, such as Prince Rupert's Regiment of Foot, had flags following rare or one-off systems of their own.

Cavalry standards, or cornets, were rather smaller than the foot colours, and followed a totally different system. There is little evidence of uniformity within a regiment; instead each troop had its own cornet, often bearing a political or religious declaration, or a cartoon, sometimes ribald or libellous in content!

The Soldier's Life

The men who fought for King or Parliament did so for a variety of reasons and motives. Many of those who enlisted in the opening stages of the war did so more or less voluntarily, either from personal belief, or hopes of regular pay, loot and excitement in normally humdrum lives. Others of course, went to the wars at the behest of their masters or employers, and although conscription was not at first formally used, many in practice had little choice in the matter.

Most of the bright hopes of the early volunteers were speedily disillusioned ; the war proved to be prolonged instead of the one decisive battle which most had expected. Though regular rates of pay were laid down, the soldier and his wage seldom came together, and both sides quickly resorted to a system of free quarter to maintain their forces. Loot and excitement also came the soldier's way much less frequently than many had imagined. Instead, sickness and wounds took a fearsome toll. Such matters as basic camp hygiene were largely ignored, and the result were outbreaks of plague and disease such as those which devastated Essex's Army in the spring of 1643. The fate of those wounded in action was also likely to be grim, given the rough and ready surgery which was the most likely to be available.

As a result of these factors, and the on-going high levels of desertion, maintaining the strength of the armies was an continuing problem. In general, it proved easier to keep the horse up to strength; many of the cavalrymen were somewhat more motivated than their comrades on foot- there were more volunteers. The horse were also in a better position to benefit from such plunder as was available and the best quarters. Some Regiments, such as those of Prince Rupert and Oliver Cromwell, were kept up to strength as a result of the prestige of their commanders. Others, such as those commanded by the near-bandit Royalist, Sir William Vaughan, "the Devil of Shrawardine", and the notorious Jonas Van Druske, attracted those with more dubious motives.

By 1644, both sides were employing a variety of expedients to recruit their armies, particularly the foot. Conscription was widely used, and was seen as an opportunity by the local authorities who administered it to rid themselves of the more undesirable elements in their local communities. Deserters were also rounded up and sent back again, so that it must have been quite common for one man to be re-enlisted several times.

Both sides enlisted enemy prisoners, who were usually willing enough to join up, given the alternative of mouldering in some plague-ridden prison. This is one reason for the comparative rarity of fights to the death and "last stands". Certainly by the later years of the war, many of the soldiers were hardened realists with no intention of pointlessly sacrificing their lives for a distant King or Parliament. By the end of the war, the New Model Army, by no means initially the band of religiously inspired idealists sometimes suggested, was made up of the remains of Parliament's old armies, plus large numbers of conscripts and former Royalist soldiers. Its success was owed to the

tradition of victory which it built up, after a shaky start, under Fairfax and Cromwell, and Parliament's relative success in keeping it supplied and paid until the war had been won.

Not to be forgotten is the part played in the war by women. Well-known are the "heroines" of the war, such as Queen Henrietta Maria- "the She-Generalissima"- and redoubtable defenders of their homes such as Lady Brilliana Harley and the Countess of Derby. But besides these there were the thousands from more humble origins; the wives and "camp-followers" who accompanied their men on campaign, and on occasion, like the unfortunate Welsh and Irish women in the Royalist camp at Naseby, paid for it with their lives.

Equally deserving of remembrance are those who stayed at home. Speaking for all of them is a London housewife, whose husband, Robert, in the Trained Bands, may well have been killed at the First Battle of Newbury.

"Most dear and loving husband, my king love, remember unto you hoping that you are in good health as I am at the writing hereof. My little Willie has been sick this fortnight. I pray you to come home if you can come safely. I do marvel that I cannot hear from you as well other neighbours do. I do desire to hear from you as soon as you can. I pray you to send me word when you do think you shall return. You do not consider I am a lone woman. I thought you would never leave me this long together. So I rest ever praying for your safe return.

your loving wife

Susan Rodway,

ever praying for you till death I depart.

Further Reading

John Adair,
"By the Sword Divided"
Eyewitnesses of the English Civil War. 1983.

Richard Holmes and Peter Young,
"The English Civil War" 1974.

John Kenyon,
"The Civil Wars of England", 1988.

Keith Roberts
"Soldiers of the English Civil War"
1. Infantry , 1989.

John Tincey,
"Soldiers of the English Civil War" 2. Cavalry. 1989.

Partizan Press
26, Cliffsea Grove, Leigh on Sea, Essex, SS9 1NQ, publish
a wide range of material relating to the English Civil War.

Should the re-enactment sequences in this video inspire you to want to take part in this exciting hobby, please contact:

Crawford's Brigade, The Roundhead Association

P. Berry
61 Melrose Road, Sheffield, S3 9DN

The Duke of York's Brigade, The King's Army

Stuart Reid
21 Chirton West View, NE29 0EP

Colonel Samuel Jones Regiment, The Sealed Knot

Paul Cunningham
Fenn Cottage, Norton St. Philip, BA3 6LN

Or write care of Partizan Press,
26 Cliffsea Grove, Leigh-on-Sea, Essex SS9 1NQ
Tel: 0702 73986